NO-FLUFF
SOFT SKILLS

Based on *Soft Skills, Hard Results* by
Anne Taylor

First published in Great Britain by Practical Inspiration Publishing, 2026

© Anne Taylor and Practical Inspiration Publishing, 2026

The moral rights of the author have been asserted

ISBN 978-1-78860-904-3 (paperback)
      978-1-78860-905-0 (ebook)

All rights reserved. This book, or any portion thereof, may not be reproduced without the express written permission of the publisher.

Every effort has been made to trace copyright holders and to obtain their permission for the use of copyright material. The publisher apologizes for any errors or omissions and would be grateful if notified of any corrections that should be incorporated in future reprints or editions of this book.

EU GPSR representative: LOGOS EUROPE, 9 rue Nicolas Poussin, LA ROCHELLE 17000, France Contact@logoseurope.eu.

Want to bulk-buy copies of this book for your team and colleagues? We can customize the content and co-brand *No-Fluff Soft Skills* to suit your business's needs.

Please email info@practicalinspiration.com for more details.

Contents

Series introduction iv

Introduction 1

Day 1: Make soft skills your business advantage 6

Day 2: Build self-awareness that drives impact 16

Day 3: Take control of how you show up 33

Day 4: Use feedback as a leadership tool 44

Day 5: Coach instead of command 55

Day 6: Lead through the power of story 66

Day 7: Flex your style without losing yourself 74

Day 8: Balance what you do and how you do it ... 80

Day 9: Lead with emotional courage 86

Day 10: Live and lead with purpose 93

Conclusion: Bringing it all together 101

Endnotes 103

Series introduction

Welcome to *6-Minute Smarts*!

This is a series of very short books with one simple purpose: to introduce you to ideas that can make life and work better, and to give you time and space to think about how those ideas might apply to *your* life and work.

Each book introduces you to ten powerful ideas, but ideas on their own are useless – that's why each idea is followed by self-coaching questions to help you work out the 'so what?' for you in just six minutes of exploratory writing. What's exploratory writing? It's the kind of writing you do just for yourself, fast and free, without worrying what anyone else thinks. It's not just about getting ideas out of your head and onto paper where you can see them; it's about finding new connections and insights as you write. This is where the magic happens.

Whatever you're facing, there's a *6-Minute Smarts* book just for you. And once you've learned how to coach yourself through a new idea, you'll be smarter for life.

Find out more...

Introduction

You care about results. You get things done. You're successful. You lead with your head – rational, analytical and logical. You're a results-focused leader. It's worked... so far.

However, when it comes to engaging, motivating and inspiring your teams, you know that you would benefit from leading more from your heart – emotional, collaborative, vulnerable and courageous. You might even have had feedback that you could be warmer, more people-oriented or more empathetic in your interpersonal interactions. And now you're ready to tackle that, effectively and efficiently.

Why does this matter? Because your organization, and by extension you, face an exhausting list of challenges that demand a different way of leading:

- Rising intergenerational differences in the workforce
- Increasing stress and emotions among staff
- Escalating speed and uncertainty of technology, competition, regulation and consumer needs
- Trying to achieve more with less.

Soft skills can address all these challenges. The practical principles in this book, when applied, practised and honed, can improve your effectiveness, impact and results. They're especially important when decisions need to be nuanced and certainty is replaced by ambiguity or relentless change.

Soft skills are people skills – not hard or technical skills like accountancy or engineering. Hard skills enable delivery of output; however, whether what you produce is successful is determined by soft skills: working with clients or managing your supply chain, negotiating changes, agreeing solutions, managing conflict, keeping everyone committed to the project. These are the behaviours we use when interacting with other people. You might not think of them as skills though (yet). You might feel they are just what you do to communicate and relate with others, be it your family, friends or work colleagues.

Introduction

Nonetheless, your ability to get results is tied to your ability to connect with others.

What you say and how you say it will have an impact on other people and the result you get. If you behave in a skilful way when interacting with others, you'll create the impact you want and improve the likelihood of getting the result you want. The good news is that research has shown that people skills, or emotional intelligence, which is the broader domain that is explained below, can be learned and developed.

Soft skills aren't fluffy. The cost of underdeveloped people skills is inefficiency and lost productivity. Conversely, the upside is increased productivity, engagement and often satisfaction. This book will help you balance your head-smart strengths through simple tools, frameworks and exercises challenging you to become more heart-smart for the benefit of the business, your team and yourself.

Soft skills have their roots in Emotional Intelligence or EI (sometimes called EQ to complement IQ). EI is the overarching term to describe four concepts: the ability to know one's emotions, manage one's emotions, understand the emotions of other people and manage relationships with others. As the *English Oxford Living Dictionary* defines it: 'The capacity to be aware of, control, and express one's emotions, and to handle interpersonal relationships judiciously and empathetically.' The concept was popularized in the 1996 book *Emotional Intelligence* by Daniel Goleman, still a great reference to this day.

EI: Emotional Intelligence		
	SELF	OTHER
KNOWING	**Self-Awareness** Knowing one's emotions	**Social Awareness** Recognizing emotions in others
DOING	**Self-Management** Managing one's emotions Motivating oneself	**Social Management** Handling relationships, interactions with others

Knowing on its own isn't enough to have great EI. You must risk putting it into practice daily to be great at it. This book will touch on all four aspects of EI to the extent necessary for you to benefit and see results while still being able to do your day job.

Introduction

This book will guide you through ten core practical skills needed to connect, influence and get results. Each day is built on direct challenges and exercises to accelerate your growth, grounded in research and real-life experience.

It's a practical guide to understanding and using people skills – or soft skills – in the workplace, and outside work if you want. It's designed to be as practical as possible, for maximum understanding and application in minimal reading time.

Whether you want to advance your career, improve your team's results or simply make work more fulfilling, these ten days will challenge you to notice, experiment and reflect. Your career advancement and business results are determined more by how you do what you do, rather than just what you get done – this is truer the higher in the organization you climb.

Lean into the challenges, set aside time each day to reflect on the 'So what...?' questions and then practise, practise, practise the tips and frameworks. It's going to feel uncomfortable and awkward; everything does at first. And it's worth it: these simple principles have the potential to transform your leadership and your fulfilment and the rewards – for you, your teams and your business – are real and lasting.

Day 1
Make soft skills your business advantage

Business is fundamentally about people. If you want to get the best out of your team, developing your soft skills will help you get better results, faster. Soft skills are not a distraction from real work – they are the foundation for how work gets done, the driver of business advantage and the essential lever for getting hard results.

The impact of soft skills is both obvious and measurable. Let's look at the facts.

The tangible cost of soft skills

Imagine you have a manager in an open-plan office criticizing one of their employees for five minutes.

Make soft skills your business advantage

How long do you think that employee will be demotivated or unproductive for? How long do you think the others in the office will be unproductive (trying to console the employee or criticizing the manager)? Imagine this manager does this every day – that's a massive productivity cost!

I call this monetizing soft skills – figuring out the monetary value of a leader's people skills. In the situation above, for example:

How often do they do this a day? 4 times a day

How many days per week do they do this? 5 times a week (daily)

How many people are in the office? 15 people

How long do you think those 15 people are thrown off by the negativity? 5 minutes each

How many weeks per year do they do this? (excluding vacation) 46 weeks

So, for 15 people losing five minutes each, 4 times per day, 5 days a week, 46 weeks: 69,000 minutes/year lost

Average salary of the employees in that space: $50,000/year or $0.401/minute

Let's be conservative and divide the impact in half – 50%

Lost productivity: ($0.401/minute x 69,000 minutes x 50%): $13,834/year.

This example quantifies the tangible cost of poor people skills. It does not quantify the increase in productivity of good or excellent people skills. The calculation could be done for positive skills when people are inspired or routinely motivated; it's just harder to do, and it feels more subjective. There's a positive upside for soft skills too – imagine the impact on productivity of an individual or team when you acknowledge someone's strong contribution.

Most managers don't stand in the middle of the office berating their staff every day. More typically they just don't know how to engage and motivate their teams. The biggest opportunity to positively add to the bottom-line is training up the managers who simply do nothing because they don't know what to do.

Humans: emotional beings capable of incredible things

Humans are emotionally driven even in business, no matter how much we like to believe that business is 'rational and factual'. The reason is that we are complex beings of physical, energetic and chemical systems that create our experience of life. Add time (evolutionary and individual) to that, and the complexity increases.

Evolution of the brain

Technology is not the only change going on; humans continue to evolve. Evolution does not necessarily mean we get better, it means we adapt better to our environment. Our brains continue to evolve and as a result have both primitive and advanced elements. The brain can be divided into three basic parts:

1. **Reptilian** (as this part is found in reptiles too): this is the primitive part, focused exclusively on survival. It does not think, it reacts. This is where the pre-programmed responses of fight, flight and freeze reside.
2. **Limbic system** (shared with other mammals): this is the centre for emotions, memories, feelings and motivations. The amygdala is a small segment of the brain located here. When we are at the mercy of the fight or flight response from the reptilian brain or intense emotions from the limbic system, Daniel Goleman refers to this as an 'amygdala hijack'. In an amygdala hijack

we react on autopilot unless the neocortex intervenes.

3. **Neocortex**: this is where we process abstract thought, logic and words. It's this area of the brain that can override the emotions of the other two parts of the brain. This is the place of choice.

The brain consists of the left hemisphere and right hemisphere. We use both parts of our brains; however, many people have a left–right hemisphere predisposition largely from birth and reinforced by early upbringing.

- **Right hemisphere.** Freedom, open, broader focus, alertness, intuition, newness, pictures, learns by body movement, a parallel processor, the present moment, part of a bigger whole.
- **Left hemisphere.** Narrow focus, attention to detail, language, reason, logic, structure, analysis, linear orientation, a serial processor, the past and the future, the voice in your head.

Information from our five senses (touch, taste, sight, sound and smell) is transmitted through our nervous system to the brain via the brain stem. The brain stem is located at the back of the brain which means that nerve sensations physically hit the emotional space of the brain, the limbic system, first before getting to the higher reasoning part of the brain near the forehead, which is why emotions are always present first when we take in stimuli. It's the communication between these two parts of our brain that is the physical source of emotional intelligence, according to Travis Bradberry and Jean Greaves in *The Emotional Intelligence Quick Book*.

Leadership is about relationships

Most problems in work situations are a result of human interactions rather than work tasks. If you think that's a bold statement, consider the times in your career that have been fulfilling, that felt easy and seemed to be less stressful. Often, they will be the times when the relationships were working well, when you enjoyed the people you were working with and there were few 'difficult interactions or characters'.

Most people quit their job because of a manager rather than an organization, as Forbes noted in 2015: 'People leave managers not companies.' The relationship with their manager is more relevant than the company values, the work they perform or the output of the company when it comes to whether someone stays or not.

As managers get promoted to increasing levels of responsibility, their jobs change and so do the skills required. I have often worked with technical leaders who found when they got promoted that they no longer coded or programmed or ran experiments or designed machinery; rather they dealt with the people doing the tasks they once loved. Their responsibilities became about setting the goals and supporting and facilitating others to achieve goals. The work of a leader becomes influencing, supporting, inspiring, clearing barriers and navigating organizational structures and differing priorities, which is all about relationships and people.

So what? Over to you...

1. Where does your team lose time, energy or engagement because of people issues?

2. What could be gained by addressing those patterns?

Make soft skills your business advantage

3. What one action could you take this week to lead the change?

Day 2
Build self-awareness that drives impact

You need to understand the emotional realm of your employees and the work environment (or so you've been told) and that starts with understanding *yourself* first – reflecting on you. This is not necessarily something you are used to or familiar with and it's probably not within your comfort zone. Don't worry; there will be clear questions and practical exploration coming up, not just airy-fairy blah blah blah.

Today is all about putting the focus on yourself; understanding everything you know about you and then reflecting on it to identify who you are at your

Build self-awareness that drives impact

core and hence what you bring to the world (and to those with whom you interact). You can't realistically head to a destination, like Switzerland, without knowing that you are starting that trip from London or Toronto. Just like at work you can't hit the sales target for the year if you don't know the current sales figures. Self-awareness is a fundamental baseline if you are going to develop your skills.

It's important to know about you as you are the constant in every interaction you have. By knowing yourself you'll have one side of that interaction figured out, at least to some degree.

By the end of today you will have accumulated and consolidated a variety of observations about you, both from your own perspective and from the perspectives of others. Your starting point will be the things you already know about yourself or have been told by others; this is the low-hanging fruit. If you've been on any leadership development or training courses, you'll probably have assessments and learning outcomes that you can reference. Once you've done that, we'll go beyond the known, or obvious, to explore the new and unknown and help you uncover motivators, preferences and aspects of yourself of which you may not currently be aware.

The Johari Window

A simple framework for what you're about to embark on is the Johari Window. It's a simple two-by-two model created by psychologists Joseph Luft and Harrington Ingham in 1955 and is useful for self-awareness and understanding relationships to others.

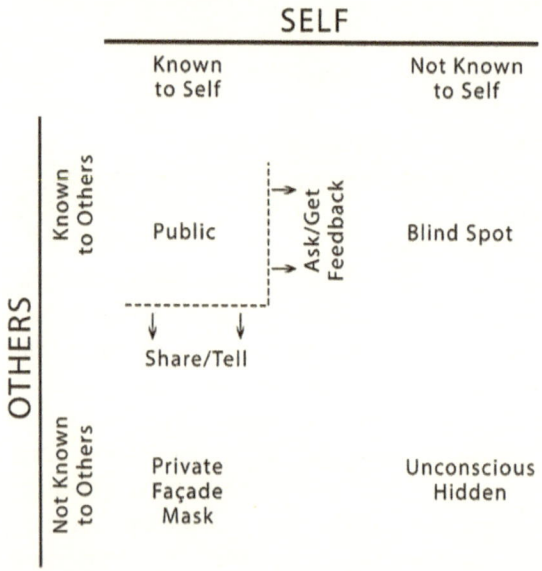

Build self-awareness that drives impact

You can use this simple framework as you pull together all the data about yourself that we're going to cover in this chapter.

Gathering your existing self-data

Start by taking an inventory of all the available data you have on yourself. Look for all the evidence you have accumulated from recent years, including:

- Performance reviews
- 360° surveys (surveys that your boss, team and peers have completed on you)
- Awards and certifications
- Complaints or criticisms
- What are your passions? What do you enjoy doing?
- Any feedback you've received, e.g. verbal accolades, congratulatory cards, letters and emails
- Any assessments you've had done such as the Myers-Briggs Type Indicator (MBTI), DISC Workplace Profile, Discovery Insights, The Leadership Circle, Hogan, Belbin Team Roles Assessment, Point Positive, Realize2 Strengths, Gallup Strengths Finder,

Enneagram. (If you don't have many of these types of assessment you can find some of them online with free or inexpensive versions to complete)
- Comments from your friends and family (yes, really!)

If you don't have any of the above, then send a simple email to a variety of personal and professional contacts asking them for input. You can use the following verbatim to make it fast and easy for yourself – don't overthink it:

> I am working on my leadership development (always a work in progress I feel) and would genuinely appreciate your input. Would you please respond to the following four questions with as much detail or specificity as you can (bearing in mind, your initial, quick response is best for both you and me):
>
> 1. What should I start doing?
> 2. What should I stop doing?
> 3. What should I continue doing?
> 4. What is unique about me versus other leaders/people you know or work with?
>
> Thank you so much for your feedback.

Build self-awareness that drives impact

(NB As a bonus, the above model of start/stop/continue is a great way of asking for feedback. It gives people specific areas to think about rather than just 'how am I doing?' or 'give me some feedback'. Keep to the start/stop/continue sequence as it makes it easier for the respondent to start the exercise and allows them to finish on a positive, so they don't feel bad.)

With regard to your friends and family, what comments would your partner or family members make about your strengths, weaknesses and that funny little quirk (potentially annoyance) that makes you distinctly you? What's the thing they tease you about? Extend that inquiry to your close friends, especially your best friend.

If the comments of your personal and professional contacts are similar, that's not surprising; it means that at your core you're one person, operating in two different environments. However, if the comments of personal and professional contacts are radically different, what does that mean for you? What's happening inside you that leads to that distinction between your work and family personas?

From all the data/input above, start to classify the following:

- What are your strengths?
- What are your weaknesses?

- What makes you unique or distinct versus other individuals?
- What interests you most in life? In your work?
- What are your preferences for communicating? Decision making? Re-energizing? Perceiving the environment around you?

Take a stab at this summary; it doesn't have to be perfect or 100% complete. Done is better than perfect (as my book coach said before my first draft of this book). This is a work in progress, just as you are. As you go through the next phases you'll enhance this with the new learnings you glean about yourself.

The personal and professional identity narrative

Another great source of information can be gleaned from a PPIN for yourself – personal and professional identity narrative. Jack Wood, IMD Professor and Jungian Analyst, encourages MBAs and Executives to do this exercise for some of their greatest learning from the programme (a bold claim considering they were paying tens of thousands of euros). The PPIN is your life story – where you have come from, where you are right now and the general trajectory of where you are headed or where you think you might be

Build self-awareness that drives impact

headed. He says, 'If you take the PPIN seriously, the process of reflecting and writing about your life – the sources of your identity and the objectives that you embrace – can help you better understand the deeper currents and patterns in your life and their continued influence.'[1]

Step 1 involves writing about the significant events in your life. Just start. This is just a collection of small stories, like chapters or simply paragraphs. You'll want to cover your childhood (not just the facts, include also your sense of what it was like growing up), school experiences, work and career (it's not a CV/resumé though), relationships (parental, romantic, friends), what have been the highlights, the low points, the regrets (of what you've done or haven't done), the times of greatest learning and when things have felt effortless. Don't worry about whether it makes sense, is well written or in a logical format. This is only for you to read and analyse. Include examples, rich descriptions (not PowerPoint or bullet points) and your feelings and emotional reactions to the events and people.

Step 2 is the analysis of what you've written. The informative part happens during the reflection. This might be while you are writing it or once it's written; when the patterns and themes in your life emerge (or appear once you observe your story on paper at a distance). What have you noticed about what you've created in your life? What's been easy? What's been hard? What has impacted you from one situation to another situation? What did you conclude about yourself or the way life works from the various events in your life? Where does it point you to in terms of further personal development? What patterns are influencing you?

Values – uncovering what matters most

Most organizations and companies have values. You can usually find them listed on a company's website or in the induction materials as a new hire. Just as a company has values that help define it and how it operates, individuals do too. Often our values are in line with those of the company we work for, whether we've consciously evaluated that fit or arrived at it unconsciously.

Values are a big part of who you are. Living your values makes you come alive; it's often when you feel 'in flow' in your life, when you're most satisfied. To determine your values, as a coach I would look for moments when you are exhibiting resonance about your life, when you are feeling the excitement, aliveness, vibration and sheer energy associated with being alive.

An exercise to enable you to discover your values

Answer the following 14 questions below.[2] You don't have to answer them all, unless you want to. The key is in the description, the 'why' rather than the 'what' – the answer itself. I'll illustrate with two client examples. One client said they loved fondue because a fondue involves sharing with others, is social, slow, as it takes time, and consists of simple ingredients, and it is a ritual, rather than the mere fact they like melted cheese. Conversely, another client liked Thai food because of its variety, spice, exotic origins and because he only has it on special occasions. The contrast of these two descriptions points to very different values between these two clients.

1. Describe a peak experience or a moment in time that was especially rewarding or poignant – be specific.
2. What is your favourite food? Favourite meal? What is it about that food or that meal that you love?
3. What is your favourite movie? Favourite book? Again, what is it about that movie you like? That book?

4. Who do you admire – dead, alive, real, fictitious – that you've known or never met? Why?
5. Describe a great day. It doesn't have to be a realistic narrative. Give your imagination free rein.
6. What do you despise? The opposite is probably a value.
7. What is your dream?
8. What was your childhood dream?
9. What must you have in your life? And why?
10. What inspires you?
11. Think of a recent important decision you made. What values were involved? What were you contributing?
12. Look at times when you overcame fear. What helped you?
13. When you are out in the daily world, what makes you smile?
14. What makes you jealous? It's probably something that you want for yourself.

The key to this exercise is to reflect on each answer and, once you've given it, look for the underlying factor that's important. Feel 'when the energy is resonant', which will mean it's important. Look for the common elements in your answers to these questions. What are the patterns or repetitive themes that arise? Circumstances do not equal values. In other words, 'family' is a circumstance. What is it about family that matters to you? What about 'family' brings you alive and energetic? It might be love, connection, legacy, community, safety or something else.

Of note, values can have a dark side. 'Love' is wonderful in terms of warmth, care and connection. Yet if you love someone too much it can dominate your life, create unhealthy dependence and even suffocate you or the person you love.

Once you've started identifying the themes, patterns and repeating words, then group similar words or themes together to create value strings, since one word is not enough to communicate the full idea or essence. For example:

> Integrity/honesty/walk the talk vs
> Integrity/whole/congruent
> Leadership/collaborative/empower vs
> Leadership/decisive/powerful

How values manifest in work and life

A sense of strong emotions is an indicator that values are present. It doesn't matter whether it's a positive/light emotion or a negative/dark emotion. Of note, no emotion is really positive or negative; these are just labels by which we judge them. Your emotional response is the signal that a value you hold is being honoured or dishonoured. If you are frustrated or angry, the chances are that a value, something that is dear to you, is being dishonoured or stepped on. If you feel joy or fulfilment, the chances are that a value is being honoured.

Hopefully by now you at least have a rudimentary sketch of you as an individual with all your uniquenesses and complexities. What you capture here will be expanded on and used in the next principle on self-awareness and self-management.

The challenge

The purpose of this challenge is to know yourself better; to be more conscious of your motivations, preferences and behaviours; to make your unconscious habits or default reactions more conscious.

Spend one hour this week pulling together all the data you have about you: performance reviews, assessments, feedback, stop/start/continue – and list your strengths, weaknesses, unique qualities and preferences. You can use the Johari Window framework if that helps you.

Build self-awareness that drives impact

Spend another hour completing the values exercise as described above. What are the themes or patterns that emerge for you? Turn them into four to seven value strings/descriptions that capture what is important to you (remember, 'done is better than perfect').

Using these as a starting point, write down a minimum of ten learnings or insights about yourself. Focus on the positives or observational commentary rather than making value judgements (good or bad).

If you have more time and want to go deeper, write your PPIN (Personal and Professional Identity Narrative) for a few hours this month – make it enjoyable. Perhaps this is an exercise you might complete down at the pub, at a café, or in the garden or another place you enjoy.

So what? Over to you...

1. What did you learn about yourself?

2. What do you need to still learn or want to learn about yourself?

3. Which of your values feel most alive in your daily work, and where might you want to express them more?

Day 3
Take control of how you show up

Self-awareness is often the first aspect of EI because without knowing yourself it's difficult to know others and therefore even harder to navigate between you and them. The first step is to notice how you respond or react to the various stimuli you encounter.

The areas outlined below of physical, emotional and intellectual observations are not an exhaustive list. They describe three main areas of stimuli and sources of learnings, rather than anything more exhaustive. This book is a practical guide for people skills and hence the focus is on the major areas rather than subtler points you might get from a full-blown EI book.

Physical – notice bodily sensations

The easiest way to notice your reactions is to tune into the feelings or sensations in your body. This seems illogical in a work context. You might wonder, what does your body have to do with work and soft skills? Actually, the physical sensations in your body are data points that you can then analyse. For example, knots in your stomach can be an early warning alert for a bad situation. Tension in your neck can indicate stress before you are conscious of it.

Each person has their own physical sensations that indicate fear, confidence, happiness, anxiety or sadness. Knowing how your body feels, noticing the physical sensations you are experiencing, often gives a heads-up that something is wrong, uncomfortable or positive.

Emotional – notice emotions

Notice your emotions or feelings. What are your emotional reactions to people, situations, information, and even to your own thoughts? What brings you joy? When do you feel love? What are you afraid of? What do you feel guilt or shame about and what makes you angry or causes pain? Your emotions are just another data set to teach you about yourself.

Take control of how you show up

When I ask new clients how they are feeling, I often get responses such as 'fine', 'OK' or 'good'. These are not emotions and are often little more than socially acceptable responses before moving on to the 'real' topic of conversation such as what work needs to be done. Pia Mellody of The Meadow Treatment Centre theorizes that there are eight basic emotions: anger, fear, pain, joy, passion, love, shame and guilt.[3] Other emotional experts agree that there are a finite number of fundamental human emotions. I find the simplicity of so few emotions helpful for novices as it simplifies the choice and it's helpful for experts to get to the root feeling. Sometimes the nuances of language can mask, deny or diffuse an emotion to the point of rendering it unrecognizable. At other times the nuances of language can provide greater specificity. For example, saying 'I feel content' is very different from saying 'I feel joyful.' For me, the energy associated with each of these words is different.

Managing emotion is an area that didn't come naturally to me. When I was younger I was hardly aware of my emotions. I grew up in a quiet, rational, non-emotional family. I was an introverted, studious, fearful child. This continued through much of my early adult life. I even picked a life partner who had been raised similarly, where you don't delve into your emotions and everything appears calm on the surface. My emotions were there when I look back; I just lacked the vocabulary to label them or the environment in which to discuss them.

I identified that I lived in fear when I was in my thirties and then tried to avoid feeling it. I still didn't have the language to articulate it and it wasn't until my parents' deaths that I really delved into the realm of emotions. Their deaths, within months of each other, broke me open. Now I know that feelings or emotions are often strong guiding forces when I am making decisions or assessing my experience in life. When I go on a date I notice how I feel when I am around the man. Do I feel confident, smart and adventurous, or cautious and scared, or bored and indifferent? How I feel when I'm with someone or in a particular situation is a great source of insight into how I view the world.

Try not to judge your emotions, simply start by noticing them and then perhaps noticing what meaning you attribute to them.

Intellectual – notice your thoughts

Our mind generates thoughts, that's its job. It constantly assesses the environment and makes meaning of it. Sometimes we are conscious of this meaning, often we're not. Where there are gaps in our information, our minds fill them in for us to make meaning. Often those meanings are assumptions as we don't always have all the information. Our minds make up stories all the time to create meaning and understanding in our lives.

Another aspect of your thoughts to notice is the critical voice in your head, the judgemental voice whispering, 'You aren't good enough' or 'Who do you think you are?' This voice is often called the saboteur because it can sabotage your efforts; it can hold you back or make you doubt yourself excessively. It comes from your past, your conditioning at home, in school or previous work. If you want to investigate its origins, therapy can help you do that. There are times when this saboteur voice is beneficial, when it protects you from failing, from looking stupid, risking or making a mistake. It tries to keep you safe. It's a defence mechanism.

The problem with it is that when you start trying new things and moving outside your comfort zone, your internal voice may not realize you are intentionally trying something new. Hence, your critical voice is conflicting with your desire to grow. It wants to keep you safe and small, to keep you in your comfort zone, to maintain the status quo. Sometimes when I hear that voice asking, 'Who do you think you are?', I remind myself that the critical voice is a sign I'm stretching myself, which allows me to keep the voice at bay.

Watch yourself while you are *doing* something (chairing a meeting, disciplining your child, cooking dinner) – notice your thoughts, behaviours and reactions. Notice the running commentary you have in your head about yourself. What are your dominant scripts? Which usually comes first for you? The thought? The feeling? The physical sensation? The more you notice, the more self-aware you will become.

Skilful self-management

You've now noticed some things about yourself. The next step is to manage yourself better. Self-management helps you to make the impression you want to make and have the impact you want to have. Self-management is the ability to respond rather than react. It's literally managing yourself, managing the time and space between what happens inside yourself, based on some stimulus, and what you put out externally. Self-management happens between the physical sensations felt in your body/ your emotions/the thoughts in your head (which could have been stimulated by a third party) and your subsequent behaviours or actions. We are responsible for our reactions; we are 'response-able' rather than at the mercy of our reptilian or limbic systems (fight, flight or freeze). We can reflect on our emotions, sensations and thoughts and decide how to respond, and the simplest way to start is simply to breathe, to hit the pause button, calm the amygdala hijack and move from an instinctive reaction to a conscious response.

Step into fully conscious choice

This is an extension of self-management. Conscious choice is about choosing consciously. It's about choosing your response, your decision, your behaviour with full awareness that it's your choice.

Conscious choice isn't just about deciding something and getting on with it. It is about realizing the power you have with every choice you make. There's a freedom and responsibility to choosing. At the extreme you have a choice in each moment, you can choose what you do or say at every instance and you are responsible for the choices you make. That responsibility means you are committing to something and often someone; there's no turning back. There's integrity about following through.

The challenge

Spend one week noticing your default reactions – physical, emotional and mental – in various situations at work. Capture your observations in a journal or note-taking app. When do you react out of habit? When do you choose your response? How does it feel different? What's the impact on your interactions and your results?

Take control of how you show up

So what? Over to you...

1. What patterns do you notice in your reactions?

2. How does increased self-awareness change your sense of agency and impact at work?

Take control of how you show up

3. How does shifting to conscious choice affect the outcomes of your interactions?

Day 4
Use feedback as a leadership tool

Giving feedback is about putting your attention on another person – a team member, employee, peer or even boss – noticing the other person's behaviours, qualities and/or results, and then actually communicating those specific observations to that individual for their growth. Feedback is a crucial leadership tool – not just a process or a box-ticking exercise. It's how you strengthen performance, grow talent and build trust, *if* it's done right.

Giving feedback

Feedback is a powerful way to help someone see their impact, develop new skills and create a stronger team. Yet for many managers and leaders, it can feel awkward, confrontational or simply uncomfortable. The intention of feedback is to help people improve – to keep doing what's working and change what isn't.

Feedback is information – about behaviour, impact, results – intended to support learning and growth. When it's delivered well, feedback can motivate, clarify expectations and reinforce what's going well.

Many managers avoid giving feedback because they fear conflict, worry about damaging relationships or just feel unprepared. Sometimes feedback is given only when things go wrong, creating a culture of fear or avoidance. Positive feedback – noticing and naming what's working – is just as important and often overlooked.

Why feedback matters

Feedback is the mechanism for improvement. If people don't know what they're doing well or where they can do better, how can they develop? When feedback is specific, timely and delivered with care, it builds trust. When feedback is absent or clumsy, people feel lost, undervalued or misunderstood.

Feedback, given skilfully, helps people learn faster, make better decisions and stay engaged. It's how you help people connect their efforts to outcomes. It can also address misunderstandings early, before they escalate.

Using a feedback model

One practical way to give feedback is to use a model. Models help you focus on behaviour and impact, rather than on personality. Here's a simple framework developed by executive coach Anna Carroll in her book *The Feedback Imperative*:

The COIN feedback model

	Description	Example of how to communicate
C	What situation or circumstance has prompted this feedback? Where was the individual? When did it occur?	At the meeting this morning... Yesterday in the office... On the phone Monday...

Use feedback as a leadership tool

	Description	Example of how to communicate
O	What did you observe? What specific action or behaviour have you seen or heard at the given moment? What did the person do or say on which you want to give feedback?	When you did... When you said... When you didn't say/do... What I observed was... What I saw was... I noticed...
I	What impact did that action or behaviour have on you, others, the business or in the room? This can be tangible like someone walking out of a meeting or intangible like a feeling.	The impact of that was... The effect of that was... The result was... It made me/others feel... It caused... I felt... The team felt...
N	What is the desired next step you would like the recipient to do with the feedback? What behaviour or action would you like them to do in the future?	Next time I suggest you... What I would want you to do is... My advice would be... In the future you could try... My preference would have been... I encourage you to...

The COIN feedback model in action

	Example of positive feedback	Example of constructive feedback
C	In today's project review meeting...	When I was walking around the floor this afternoon...
O	I noticed when Marc expressed his concern over the launch timing you paused, nodded your head, asked a couple of open-ended questions and asked, 'This sounds important to you, can we set up some separate time to discuss it?'	I saw you leaning over your sales manager advising him that he could have been more structured when answering the customer's questions in the customer meeting this morning.
I	When you listen to people, ask clarifying questions, acknowledge someone, even if junior to you – Marc feels more valued, the idea of raising concerns is encouraged thereby mitigating risks, and others in the meeting respect you even more.	The impact on him could have been embarrassment and intimidation. And because you are a manager, others in the open-plan office might have felt uncomfortable and that you were being disrespectful.

Use feedback as a leadership tool

	Example of positive feedback	Example of constructive feedback
N	Well done. Keep up the good work. Thanks for role-modelling those skills to the attendees.	In the future, please deliver constructive feedback eye-to-eye and ideally in your office. It's better to be on 'the same level' and to punish in private and praise in public.

You can download a template for a COIN discussion from my website at: https://directions-coaching.com/wp-content/uploads/2020/08/Directions_Coin-Feedback_Revised.pdf

How you give feedback is vital if it's to be received well.

- **Feedback should be timely.** As close as possible to the event, so it's relevant and actionable.
- **Feedback should be regular.** Not just at performance reviews; as part of your ongoing leadership.

Feedback conversations are two-way. Invite feedback from others. Ask, 'What could I do differently?' or 'What do you need more or less of from me?' When you model receiving feedback, you show it's safe to learn and grow.

The experience of feedback

Receiving feedback can be just as challenging as giving it. Most people feel vulnerable or exposed when they hear feedback, even when it's positive. It's natural to feel defensive or want to explain or justify your actions.

The key is to listen, stay open and reflect before responding. Try to separate the message from your emotional reaction. Ask clarifying questions if needed. Say thank you. Use feedback as a mirror, not a verdict.

Leaders who develop the skill of both giving and receiving feedback create a culture of learning. Over time, this raises performance across the team or organization.

The challenge

Spend one week practising the feedback model above. Each day, give at least one piece of specific, behaviour-based feedback to a colleague, peer or team member. Notice how it feels for you and for them.

Use feedback as a leadership tool

Ask for feedback yourself at least once this week. Use a question like, 'What's one thing I could do differently to help our work together?' Capture what you hear, how you feel and how you respond.

So what? Over to you…

1. What did you learn about your feedback habits – do you avoid it, rush it or approach it directly?

Use feedback as a leadership tool

2. What is one feedback conversation you could have this week to help someone grow?

3. What might you try next time to improve your feedback conversations?

Day 5
Coach instead of command

Many leaders are promoted because they are strong doers and problem-solvers. However as responsibilities grow, it becomes less about doing the work yourself and more about developing others to succeed.

A coaching approach shifts your focus from telling people what to do to helping them think for themselves. Telling is giving advice, instruction or direction – it's fast and sometimes necessary, especially in urgent situations. And over time, always telling can create dependency, stifle initiative and reduce engagement.

Coaching, by contrast, is slower at first and pays off in greater growth. When you coach, you trust that the other person has insights, ideas and resourcefulness – even if they need help to access it.

Both telling and coaching are important, although as most leaders know how to tell already, many need more tools and encouragement to coach, so that's what we're focusing on here. A directive approach is required in a training situation, in crisis or where safety or compliance is at stake; however, most day-to-day leadership moments offer opportunities to coach. When you see someone struggling, ask a question rather than giving the answer. When you see potential, invite them to stretch.

Coaching is not just for formal 'coaches' – it's a mindset and set of skills for every leader. When you coach, you ask questions, listen deeply and help others clarify their goals and challenges. You encourage them to reflect, consider options and decide on their own actions. Coaching builds confidence, accountability and capability.

Practical coaching skills for leaders

To coach, start with curiosity. Ask open questions:

- What options do you see?
- What's the real challenge here for you?
- How do you want to move forward?

Coach instead of command

Resist the urge to jump in with your solution. Listen longer than feels comfortable. Notice what's not being said just as much as what is. Offer support, not just direction.

Coaching can be as simple as holding a space for someone to think out loud, or as structured as a planned development conversation. Either way, the goal is to help the other person build clarity, confidence and action.

The GROW model, first published by John Whitmore in his book *Coaching for Performance* in 1992, is a widespread framework to use when coaching.[4] It might not seem sophisticated – just four simple steps – yet it can be incredibly powerful.

The GROW coaching model

Step	Explanation	Examples of actual questions to ask
Goal	What's the goal?	• What is it you would like to discuss? • What would you like to achieve? • What do you want to get from this session/conversation?

Step	Explanation	Examples of actual questions to ask
	This is to help define what, in fact, the problem or issue is. What's the objective? What are you trying to achieve or accomplish? This can take a few minutes or quite a while, depending on what clarity the employee already has.	• What would need to happen for you to walk away feeling that this time was well spent? • What do you want to be different? • What outcome do you want? • What would you like to happen that is not happening now? • What would you like not to happen that is happening now? • Is that realistic? • Can we do that in the time we have available? • Will that be of real value to you?
Reality	What's the current reality or situation?	• What is happening at the moment? • How do you know that this is accurate? • When does this happen?

Coach instead of command

Step	Explanation	Examples of actual questions to ask
	It's valuable to explore this area so the employee is very clear what is going on. This could highlight assumptions they have and gaps in knowledge – about the situation or themselves!	• How often does this happen? • What effect does this have? • How can you verify that this is so? • What have you or others done previously about this? • What other factors are relevant? • Who else is involved? • What is their perception of the situation? • What have you tried so far? What did you learn?
Options	What are the possible options?	• What are you thinking of doing? • What could you do to change the situation? • What alternatives are there to that approach?

No-Fluff Soft Skills

Step	Explanation	Examples of actual questions to ask
	This is where you want them to brainstorm about alternatives. Continue having them generate ideas until they've reasonably exhausted all the options.	• Tell me what possibilities for action you see. • What approach/actions have been used in similar circumstances? • Who might be able to help? • Would you like suggestions from me? • What are the benefits of that option? What might the problems be? • Which options are of interest to you? • Would you like to choose an option to act on?
Will or Way Forward	What's going to happen? What will you do? What's your way forward?	• What are the next steps? • When will you take them? • What might get in the way? • Do you need to capture the steps in your diary?

Coach instead of command

Step	Explanation	Examples of actual questions to ask
	This is the time to have the coachee define next steps and create accountability. What will they do? When? How will they ensure success?	• What support do you need? • How will you enlist that support? • How will you know you are making progress? • What else needs to be done?

Coaching is more than just *what* you do: asking questions, listening and following a model. It's just as much about *how* you do it. Think about how you want to be when you coach someone – present, open, suspending judgement, attentive, open to what comes up, curious, purposeful and more. It requires dancing in the moment, listening to what is said, being silent, having no preconceived notion of how the conversation will go.

The challenge

This week, choose one conversation each day where you will deliberately use a coaching approach. Instead of telling, ask questions. Listen for the other person's ideas before offering your own.

Coach instead of command

✏️ So what? Over to you…

1. When do you default to telling rather than coaching? What impact does that have?

2. How does it feel for you to coach rather than tell?

3. What difference did you notice in the other person's engagement or ownership?

Day 6
Lead through the power of story

If you've ever had feedback that you need to be more motivating or inspiring, storytelling could be the answer. Storytelling is a powerful way to connect, influence and inspire. In business, as in life, facts and data rarely persuade on their own. It's the stories we remember and repeat; the stories that move us to act.

Storytelling isn't about fiction or spinning a yarn – it's about illustrating ideas, sharing meaning and bringing data to life through lived experience. Stories help others relate to your message. They demonstrate values, provide context and turn dry concepts into something people can feel and use.

Lead through the power of story

As a leader, storytelling is a way to engage others, to create emotional connection and to make your vision real. Stories are vehicles for your message. They help people see what's possible, remember what matters and feel why it counts.

Anyone can use stories. You don't have to be a natural raconteur, performer or extrovert. You just need to pay attention to the events, moments and examples that illustrate your point.

A storytelling recipe

The secret of storytelling is simply to think of your stories before you might even need or want to share them. That's right, plan them in advance. Here's a simple, step-by-step process you can follow:

1. **Peak moments.** Think about your professional journey, the highlights, low points, key lessons learned and crossroads. Also, think about what matters to you as a leader and where that purpose or motivation came from.
2. **Your situation.** From the specific events and moments in time identified above, think about your situation – your thoughts, feelings, motivations and relationships with those involved in each of those peak moments.

3. **Lessons.** Identify the lessons you learned from each of those peak moments. In other words, what is the moral of each of your peak moments? This will become the 'so what' of your story and be useful in identifying which story to share and when to share it, so stay tuned.
4. **Choose.** Which topics or morals might be the most applicable to your current leadership situation? Which might be helpful to the challenges your team members are facing now?
5. **Create.** Take the topic or moral from above and create the story, including the situation, the learning moment, the feelings and the 'so what' or moral.
6. **Elaborate.** Put in more emotion (you probably have skimped on feelings as so many people do), share the angst and the light bulb feeling, include specific details to add flavour and paint a picture, and lastly, reveal how that transformed or impacted you from that moment on.
7. **Refine.** Delete some of the factual filler or extra words. The length of your story should be about three to five minutes. You could have a slightly longer version depending on the application.

8. **Practise.** By yourself first, read it over and feel it. Then read it out loud to hear yourself say it (you don't want the first time you hear it to be when another hears it). Then read it in front of a mirror, occasionally looking at your face in the mirror. This increases your comfort level further. Hone the message and wording, if necessary.

9. **Deliver.** This isn't about memorizing a story; it's about knowing the structure and flow of what you want to convey. Try it out with a low-risk person and use your newfound awareness-sensing skills to judge the impact. Or you could ask for feedback! Also, watch how others tell stories – what works and what doesn't for them.

The aim is to create resonance – a sense of 'I recognize that' or 'That could be me'. The best stories are simple, human and direct. They don't have to be dramatic; sometimes a small moment is the most powerful.

When to use stories in leadership

Use stories when you want to:

- Inspire action or change
- Illustrate a value or behaviour

- Explain a decision or direction
- Celebrate success or learn from failure
- Make a vision or strategy tangible.

Stories can clarify ambiguity, motivate effort and create shared understanding. When people hear a story, they connect emotionally as well as intellectually.

Pay attention to moments in your workday that could become stories. Notice challenges overcome, lessons learned or times when you saw a value in action. Collect these moments, jotting down notes or sharing them with a trusted colleague.

As you become more confident, ask others for stories, too. Leadership is not about being the only storyteller – it's about encouraging story-sharing across the team.

The challenge

Identify a message you want to communicate – a value, a learning, a vision. Find or recall a story that brings this to life. Share it with your team or a colleague. Notice their response: Did the story make your message clearer or more memorable?

Lead through the power of story

 So what? Over to you...

1. What's a story from your experience that could illustrate a key value or lesson for your team?

2. How did it feel to share a story in a work setting? What response did you notice?

Lead through the power of story

3. What did you learn about using story as a leadership tool?

Day 7
Flex your style without losing yourself

As a leader, you work with people who have different personalities, backgrounds and preferences. The ability to flex your style – to adapt how you communicate and relate – is a hallmark of EI. It doesn't mean becoming someone you're not. It's about adapting authentically.

When you adapt your style, you:
- Build stronger relationships
- Communicate more effectively
- Increase your influence and impact
- Reduce misunderstandings and conflict.

It's not about being fake or inauthentic. It's about expanding your range. Think of it like learning a new

Flex your style without losing yourself

language: you still have your native tongue, and now you can connect with more people in more ways.

Authentic adaptation means staying true to your values and core self, while being flexible in your approach. It's responding to what others need without losing your own sense of direction or integrity.

Some worry that adapting means giving in, pleasing others or becoming a chameleon. There's a difference between flexibility and compliance. Flexibility is about choice; compliance is about surrender. Adapting is about being intentional in the way you interact with the other person.

Tips on how to adapt authentically

- Notice others' preferences: Do they like detail or big picture? Fast pace or more time to process? Written or spoken communication?
- Flex your language and approach to meet them where they are.
- Use active listening: reflect back what you're hearing; clarify before responding.
- Check your intention: are you adapting to connect and serve, or out of fear or habit?
- Keep boundaries: adapt style, not core values.

Experiment with flexing your style in low-risk situations. Try matching your energy to the person you're with. Use different communication methods and notice what works. Be curious about others' reactions and adjust as needed.

The goal is not to please everyone, rather to build stronger, more effective relationships. Over time, you'll develop a wider repertoire and more confidence in your ability to connect across differences.

The challenge

Choose one relationship or interaction where you will consciously adapt your style. Try a different approach: adjust your communication, pace or method.

Flex your style without losing yourself

 So what? Over to you...

1. In what situations do you find it hardest to flex your style? Why?

2. What was the impact on the other person when you tried out adapting?

Flex your style without losing yourself

3. What did you learn about your own flexibility and authenticity?

Day 8
Balance what you do and how you do it

Leadership is rarely about simple choices. It's often about managing tensions – balancing what you do with how you do it, holding structure and flexibility, results and relationships, direction and listening.

What is balance?

Balance is about having things in the correct proportion, so the overall mix is stable rather than lopsided or unbalanced. Balance is not a static point; it's a dynamic process. As a leader, you are constantly adjusting, responding to new challenges and shifting circumstances.

Balance what you do and how you do it

To take the skills of telling and listening, for example, balance is about recognizing that you need to have a balance between those skills that's appropriate to the situation and people involved. Think about it more as a continuum, with listening at one end and telling at the other. Some situations are all about listening (a colleague's child is gravely ill), some are all about telling (there's a fire, EVACUATE IMMEDIATELY!), and most are somewhere in between – the important thing is to find the right place on that continuum.

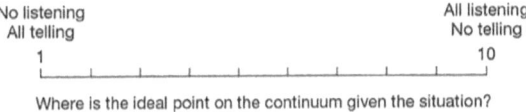

Where is the ideal point on the continuum given the situation?

Many leaders focus on tasks, outcomes and deadlines, sometimes at the expense of connection. Conversely, others that excel at building relationships may avoid difficult decisions or tough conversations. Sustainable leadership requires both: achieving results *and* nurturing the team.

How to balance

This isn't about letting go of your natural tendencies or preferences. It isn't about changing yourself. It isn't about going from one extreme to the other end of the continuum. As Dan Cable, a professor at London Business School, points out, it's about having flexibility within a frame. Define the landscape of how you want to be and what you want to create with other stakeholders and then play within that framework.[5] To balance well, start by noticing your default. Do you tend to focus on delivery and overlook relationships? Or do you spend time connecting and shy away from accountability?

Identify which tendencies are your growth opportunities. For example, if your tendency is to be task-led, your stretch zone would be relationship-led. Frame it as positive, what you want to practise, rather than what you want to avoid or not do.

Balance also means knowing your own limits and taking care of your own energy. You cannot serve others well if you are depleted. Notice when you need to step back, recharge or ask for help.

The challenge

Pay attention to a recurring tension in your leadership – perhaps between delivery and relationship, or direction and flexibility. In one meeting or interaction, pause and ask, 'What does this situation need?' Experiment with adjusting your approach.

Balance what you do and how you do it

 So what? Over to you...

1. Where did you notice the need for balance most?

2. How did your choice to adjust affect others and outcomes?

Balance what you do and how you do it

3. What's one small adjustment you can try to bring more balance to your leadership this week?

Day 9
Lead with emotional courage

Leadership is not just about strategy or skill. True leadership requires courage – especially emotional courage. It's about being willing to be vulnerable, to face discomfort and to take risks in service of something bigger.

Courage

Courage isn't the absence of fear. It's the ability to move forward with something scary despite the fear! Few of us face real physical danger in the workplace, yet we still require courage to overcome our fears. According to Inc.com,[6] imposter syndrome, the fear of being found to be incompetent is the #1 fear

Lead with emotional courage

among CEOs, and bosses are also fearful of looking stupid, appearing vulnerable, political attacks and underachieving.

In my experience, most CEOs and MDs are surprised to find that these feelings are normal; they thought it was exclusively their issue.

There are two areas for applying courage in business:

1. **Vocationally.** The courage to do things differently, to have different solutions. This is about the work itself, changing a manufacturing or IT system, changing a process, using social media and paid product placement rather than traditional 30-second TV adverts. These changes feel less risky, easier to take, requiring less personal courage.
2. **Personally.** The courage to be different, to stand out, to go against the norm, to expose one's self. This is the courage to ask the 'stupid' question, to oppose the status quo, to put your head above the parapet about a decision or defined direction. This feels scary and risky, with huge repercussions to the individual.

There is a light side and a dark side to courage, as there is to every quality. The light side is powerful, brave and expanding, and the dark side is reckless, cavalier and fool-hearted. The right kind of courage will increase your effectiveness, fulfil your potential and grow yourself on this journey of life, and it's essential for EI and personal growth.

Courage is contagious. When you show up with courage, you create space for others to do the same. Teams become more open, more resilient and more willing to tackle challenges.

Vulnerability

Vulnerability is the basis for soft skills, EI and authentic leadership. Researcher Brené Brown goes so far as saying that vulnerability is at the core of meaningful human experiences.[7] It is about exposing yourself, risking sharing something about yourself that might threaten your position or status. (NB This is very different from being weak. Weakness is about lacking power to perform or having a flaw or limitation. It's about revealing something about yourself that's personal or intimate, not flagging a shortcoming in your ability.)

Vulnerability requires trust of others and yourself. You need to trust the person with whom you are being vulnerable. You need to trust yourself that you have the courage to do it and can handle whatever happens following your revelation.

Lead with emotional courage

Courage and vulnerability are two sides of the same coin. You cannot have one without the other. Every courageous act involves vulnerability, and every vulnerable moment takes courage.

Practical ways to lead with emotional courage

- Notice where you feel discomfort or fear – that's often a sign of a growth edge.
- Take small risks: share a doubt, own a mistake, try a new behaviour.
- Model openness in meetings: invite input, acknowledge uncertainty, celebrate learning as well as success.

Courage grows with practice. Each time you act despite fear, you expand your capacity. Vulnerability builds trust, encourages others and humanizes leadership.

The challenge

Identify one situation where you can practise emotional courage – perhaps giving feedback, asking for help or speaking up about a concern. Take the risk, even if it feels uncomfortable.

So what? Over to you...

1. What was the outcome of your courageous action?

Lead with emotional courage

2. How did it feel to be vulnerable?

3. What did you learn about your own capacity for courage?

Day 10
Live and lead with purpose

As leaders, it's easy to become consumed by daily demands, urgent targets and immediate results. Yet the most powerful and lasting leadership is grounded in purpose – in knowing what matters to you and living and leading with intention.

Live a life of no regrets

This might sound overly philosophical; however, for me this is a philosophy born out of real life and death experiences. Living a life of no regrets is the epitome of no-fluff soft skills.

- You live your values and pursue a life of satisfaction in your uniquely 'you' way.

- You strive for 'clean' relationships – when things need to be said for another's benefit or for your emotional wellbeing, you have the conversation.
- You own your impact on other people and the world.
- You are courageous in your pursuits and relationships and therefore you're vulnerable.
- You balance all apparent contradictions and live with the paradoxes.
- You enjoy the journey, with one eye on creating the legacy you want.
- You realize every day could be your last.

Live a life of gratitude

Gratitude is not just an attitude, it's a practice. It's a way of noticing the good, the growth and the gifts in everything. Practising gratitude means slowing down and paying attention – to the people around you, to the progress you've made and to the opportunities you have.

Why? Multiple research sources document the benefits of gratitude across five key areas:[8]

1. **Emotional wellbeing.** Happier, less anxiety and depression, bounce back from stress.

Live and lead with purpose

2. **Physical health.** Better sleep, fewer aches and pains, less pain, more exercise.
3. **Personality.** More optimism, self-esteem, spirituality.
4. **Social interactions.** More friends, better marriages, deeper relationships.
5. **Career enhancements.** Greater networking, better teamwork, less absenteeism, greater employee and client loyalty.

Tips for living and leading with gratitude:

- Start or end your day by listing three things you're grateful for in a physical notebook – if you only 'think' about them they are just fleeting thoughts
- Be specific – the detail is what makes the experience rich and creates the good feeling
- Do it regularly, make it a habit
- Do it for at least a month as the experience (and ease of doing it) will evolve over that time. It will get easier as you train your eye and brain to see the good in the moment.

Gratitude creates resilience. When you can see what is good, even in challenge, you are better able to support others and to navigate uncertainty.

Purpose and legacy

Living and leading with purpose means clarifying what matters most – your values, your aspirations, your desired impact. Purpose doesn't have to be grand or public. It's about meaning: Why do you do what you do? What contribution do you want to make? What do you want to be remembered for?

Legacy is built one choice at a time. It's less about accomplishments and more about how you showed up, how you treated others and how you used your gifts.

As you reflect on your own journey, consider: What stories do you want to create? What regrets do you want to avoid? How can you lead with more gratitude and meaning every day?

The challenge

Take time to reflect on your purpose as a leader and as a human being. Ask yourself:

- What matters most to me?
- What do I want my legacy to be?
- Where can I practise more gratitude and live with fewer regrets?

Live and lead with purpose

Each day, write down one way you acted with purpose or appreciation. Notice how it affects your mood, your interactions and your sense of fulfilment.

So what? Over to you...

1. What would you regret not doing, saying or becoming in your leadership or life?

Live and lead with purpose

2. Where or how can you practise gratitude more intentionally – for yourself, your team or your circumstances?

3. What's one step you can take to align your actions with your deeper purpose?

Conclusion: Bringing it all together

The journey through soft skills is a journey of becoming:

- more aware
- more adaptable
- more courageous
- more purposeful.

The skills and practices in this book are not just tools for leadership – they are invitations to grow as a human being.

You have learned to build self-awareness, to take control of how you show up, to use feedback skilfully, to coach instead of command, to lead through story, to flex your style, to balance competing demands, to lead with emotional courage and to live with gratitude and purpose.

You have seen how a simple interaction, a word of appreciation or a moment of courage can ripple through a team or organization. The cost of underdeveloped people skills is inefficiency, disengagement and lacklustre results. The upside is greater productivity, innovation and satisfaction.

People skills impact every area of our lives – professional and personal. People skills impact our enjoyment of life because few of us live a completely solitary life. I hope this is a precursor to further development for you around emotions and human interactions, and if you stop here that's OK too. There is no referee sitting on the sidelines of your life judging you as pass or fail. There is no end destination of perfection, rather it's about being in the game, living the journey of life. You're going to make mistakes, you're going to feel awkward, and the key is to stay in the game and keep learning.

Enjoy the journey!

Endnotes

[1] J. Denfeld Wood. The Personal and Professional Identity Narrative (PPIN).

[2] L. Whitworth, K. Kimsey-House, H. Kimsey-House and P. Sandahl *Co-Active Coaching: Changing Business, Transforming Lives: New Skills for Coaching People Toward Success in Work and Life* (2007).

[3] P. Mellody. www.piamellody.com/articles.html

[4] J. Whitmore *Coaching for Performance* (1992).

[5] D. M. Cable *Alive at Work* (2018).

[6] Inc.com. Roger Jones, chief executive of London-based Vantage Hill Partners, study of 116 CEOs and other executives (24 February 2015).

[7] B. Brown *Daring Greatly: How the Courage to be Vulnerable Transforms the Way We Live, Love, Parent, and Lead* (2012); B. Brown *Dare to Lead* (2018).

[8] www.happierhuman.com/benefits-of-gratitude/; https://positivepsychologyprogram.com/benefits-gratitude-research-questions/

Enjoyed this?
Then you'll love…

Soft Skills, Hard Results by Anne Taylor

Business Book Awards Winner: Self Development Book of The Year 2021

Everyone says a great leader needs EQ, Emotional Intelligence, soft skills, blah, blah, blah. What does that even mean? Where do you start? Where's the line for that on the P&L?

You might think that business is all about facts and figures. You probably prefer it that way. The truth is that as uncertainty and business complexity increase, successful leaders need to embrace soft skills to get the best out of their people in a sustainable manner.

No-Fluff Soft Skills

In this succinct, no-nonsense approach, Anne Taylor shares:

- Key soft skills relevant for leadership and practical applications of how to use them every day drawn from real-life case studies
- Straightforward tools to better understand yourself, because your leadership starts with *you*
- Simple frameworks to communicate with others to get things done while building a stronger relationship with them (at the same time, how efficient!)

Logical ideas you can try immediately with online support if you want it. All done in an easy-to-read, logical, organized manner for people who prefer facts and don't consider themselves natural 'people people'.

In a direct yet professional manner, Anne combines the results-oriented focus from her extensive business background in Fortune 100 corporations with her passion for personal awareness and conscious choice to help you get better results through your people, fast.

The practical principles in this book, when applied, practised and honed, can improve your effectiveness, impact and bottom-line results.

Other *6-Minute Smarts* titles

 *Beating Burnout* (based on *The Burnout Bible* by Rachel Philpotts)

 *Building Great Teams* (based on *Workshop Culture* by Alison Coward)

 *Collaborate Better* (based on *Collabor(h)ate* by Deb Mashek PhD)

 *Customer Success Essentials* (based on *The Customer Success Pioneer* by Kellie Lucas)

 *Do Change Better* (based on *How to be a Change Superhero* by Lucinda Carney)

 *Find Your Confidence* (based on *Coach Yourself Confident* by Julie Smith)

 *Find Your Purpose* (based on *The Purpose Handbook* by Eloise Skinner)

 *Get That Promotion* (based on *Getting On* by Joanna Gaudoin)

 *Grow Your Product Business* (based on *Tame Your Tiger* by Catherine Erdly)

 *How to be Happy at Work* (based on *My Job Isn't Working!* by Michael Brown)

 *How to Get to Know Your Customer* (based on *Do Penguins Eat Peaches?* by Katie Tucker)

 *The Inclusion Mindset* (based on *Beyond Discomfort* by Nadia Nagamootoo)

 *The Listening Leader* (based on *The Listening Shift* by Janie Van Hool)

 *Love Your Job* (based on *WorkJoy* by Beth Stallwood)

 *Managing Big Teams* (based on *Big Teams* by Tony Llewellyn)

 *Mastering People Management* (based on *Mission: To Manage* by Marianne Page)

 *No Nonsense PR* (based on *Hype Yourself* by Lucy Werner)

 *Present Like a Pro* (based on *Executive Presentations* by Jacqui Harper)

 *Reimagine Your Career* (based on *Work/Life Flywheel* by Ollie Henderson)

 *Sales Made Simple* (based on *More Sales Please* by Sara Nasser Dalrymple)

 *The Speed Storytelling Toolkit* (based on *Exposure* by Felicity Cowie)

 *Stay Focused* (based on *Attention!* by Rob Hatch)

 *Write to Think* (based on *Exploratory Writing* by Alison Jones)

Look out for more titles coming soon! Visit www.practicalinspiration.com for all our latest titles.

www.ingramcontent.com/pod-product-compliance
Lightning Source LLC
Chambersburg PA
CBHW031433210526
45464CB00005B/2189